Words of Life
Daily Devotional

A SEASON
OF GRIEF

Stephanie M. White
Kathleen Higham

A SEASON OF GRIEF

A Season of Grief is a devotional that addresses the process of mourning and the effects it has on our lives. When we discuss death, we must also discuss being prepared for our own death. This devotional focuses on God's Word and His love for us. His love for us has given us everything we need to be prepared for death.

> John 3:16 NIV For God so loved the world that He gave His one and only Son, that whoever believes in Him shall not perish but have eternal life.

God's love for us provided us with Jesus Christ. Jesus Christ came to this earth and lived and died for us. His death was for us. He took our place and paid the price for our sin.

> Romans 6:23 NIV For the wages of sin is death, but the gift of God is eternal life in Christ Jesus our Lord.

You do not have to pay the price for your sin because Jesus paid that price for you. He loves you that much!

The Bible also tells us that the heart of the wise is in the house of mourning (Ecclesiastes 7:4) – this is true because a wise person recognizes death is a fact and they prepare for that time. We prepare for death by receiving the gift of Jesus Christ. Jesus Christ paid the price for our sin; He died in our place so that we could have eternal life.

> Romans 10:9-10 NIV That if you confess with your mouth, "Jesus is Lord," and believe in your heart that God raised Him from the dead, you will be saved. For it is with your heart that you believe and are justified, and it is with your mouth that you confess and are saved.

Have you received God's free gift of life? Today is the day to open your heart and receive. Pray now. Accept what Christ has done for you!

Day 1 – by Stephanie M. White

Ecclesiastes 3:1, 4 NIV
There is a time for everything, and a season for every activity under heaven…a time to weep and a time to laugh, a time to mourn and a time to dance.

There is a time to mourn and weep. We must never feel like we cannot grieve. This is a part of loss and it helps us to deal with the emotions we experience during this time.

This devotional is entitled "A Season of Grief" because of this very verse. There is a time to mourn; there is a season or an appointed time that needs to be set apart to deal with loss. This devotional will take you through fifty such days because we need to be in the habit of abiding in the Word of God.

We can ignore loss and just keep on going, but this will leave us with unresolved feelings later on. These feelings need to be addressed. Do not allow others, your flesh, or the world, to make you feel as if you have no right to grieve. There are some who even state that grieving is a lack of faith; this is false! Grieving is nothing more than experiencing great sorrow. This does not mean that we are lacking faith! It simply means that we are human and we have suffered a great loss. Faith will take us through grief, but faith does not eliminate the experience of grief. There *is* a time to grieve.

Genesis 23:2 KJV And Sarah died…Abraham came to mourn for Sarah, and to weep for her.

Biblical figures mourned loss. We cannot ignore the anguish we feel when we lose a loved one; we must address it with the Word of God. During a season of grief we must be sure to take the Word of God in regularly. Remember that we can take the Word in through the written Word, song, or the spoken Word – take it in every way you can.

As we abide in the Word, we will find ourselves leaving the confinements of grief and entering a state of joy. There is also a time for dancing!

Day 2 – by Kathleen Higham
God's Will

Lord, thank You for this moment
Even if affliction rules the day
I thank You for each breath I take
You said it would be this way.

For You have promised eternal life
But only if we walk in Your Will
And the Will of God is the Word
In Him let our hearts be still.

Close your eyes and meet with Him
Take one step through each loss
Following Him in faith and trust
Take one step back to the Cross.

For the Will of God is Salvation
So leave your old life behind
Walking with His Divine direction
And the Path of Christ you will find.

God's Will is surely a clear call
His Word is a lamp to our feet
But still we depend on our faith
Seeking Him at His Mercy Seat.

He desires that no one should perish
Be submissive and surrender your soul
Your suffering can be purposeful
His Will is the ultimate goal.

So rejoice and pray unceasingly
Then step blindly around the bend
Standing at the foot of the Cross
Where His Light shines without end.

1 Thessalonians 5:16

Day 3– by Stephanie M. White

Deuteronomy 34:8 NIV
The Israelites grieved for Moses in the plains of Moab thirty days, until the time of weeping and mourning was over.

In Deuteronomy we see that there was a time of weeping and mourning; there was a *set* time or a season. In this instance, it was thirty days. There were thirty days set aside for nothing but grieving their loss. This does not mean that we cannot mourn for longer than thirty days; it *does* mean that we cannot *live* in the grief. After this set-apart time, they were to move forward even though they were still in pain; grieving their loss would no longer be their main focus.

When we experience loss we are tempted to stand still. This temptation must be met with prayer and the Word of God. Many times we do not feel like we can pray or read when we are grieving, but that is where we will find our strength to go on. There will be a period of time when you feel immobilized; this is that set time. God wants us to understand that it is normal to grieve a loss, but He also wants us to know that this is not meant to be our way of life.

You may have lost someone years ago and you still feel as if you are in mourning; this is not unusual. A loss affects you for the rest of your life. If we are honest, things will never be the same. The loss of a loved one has an emotional impact that will never pass, but we *can* move forward.

As you read this devotional, I pray that the Word of God will inhabit your being and move you to go forward in life. This does not mean that you forget the loved one you lost, but it does mean that you cannot live in the past forever. In Christ we can overcome the debilitating power that grief can have over us and we can rejoice in the memories God has blessed us with. If your loss is significant it is because the impact they had on your life was monumental; we have much to be thankful for as we remember those we are missing. Even though our hearts are heavy, we *can* move on in life and live life to the fullest through Christ. Our loved one would want it that way.

Day 4 – by Kathleen Higham
Your Son

There is no pain as this
God knows about a Mother
A Son died on a Cross
There is no pain, no other.

All will suffer fiery trials
For a little while, God said
Grief may come and crush us
When from a loved one, life fled.

There is no pain as this
When a Mother loses a son
She falls to her knees, broken
Remembering in her womb, as one.

Tears of life dry, then end
But the memories never fade
A tiny hand rested in yours
Then a Mother was betrayed.

There is no pain as this
No answer to her prayer
Anger comes in gasping breaths
Questioning, "God do You care?"

How could this ever happen?
In your body this child grew
In a second, gone forever
The son so loved left you.

There is no pain as this
But the Mother of God, she knew
Her Son was crucified before her
She fell to her knees too.

Oh Lord, there must be peace
I pray that You draw near
Your Son, my son, together
Perfect love casts out all fear.

John 4:18

Day 5– by Stephanie M. White

Matthew 5:4 NIV
Blessed are those who mourn, for they will be comforted.

For the most part, we do not equate mourning with blessing; however, God does. This may seem like an oxymoron, but God *does* know what He is talking about.

The blessing in mourning is the comfort we can receive from God if we are willing to accept it. When we are mourning, God can speak to us in a way that we may not respond to at any other time in our lives. When we are grieving we feel broken; broken, but not beyond repair. Remember, God can do a work in us when we are at our lowest point that He may not be able to do at any other time.

"Comforted" was translated from a Greek word that means to call near. This word also means to invite, to console, to call for, and to beseech. This word demonstrates God's desire to heal our broken heart by drawing us close to Him.

If your heart is broken you may be mad at God. This feeling is real and it needs to be dealt with immediately. God is the only answer to your grief; He is the only One who can heal your broken heart. This anger we may be feeling is of the flesh and it is keeping us from God. Go to Him and talk to Him. Tell Him how you really feel. Meditate on Scripture that expresses God's love for you. Realize that you may not understand why you are suffering loss, but God does have a plan. Continue on with this devotional and discover His plan.

God wants to console you – He wants to comfort you; but, you must allow Him access into your broken heart. You are not suffering loss because God is bad; you are suffering loss because death is part of life in this fallen world (Psalm 89:48).

God is calling us near; He is inviting us to cling to Him. When we begin to answer this call, we begin to find that this is where we are meant to be at all times. Clinging to God is not just for times of grieving; clinging to God should be our way of life at all times. This lifestyle is the blessed life! The life that is dependent on Christ is blessed indeed!

Dear Friends,

When I was a very young nurse I had a friend who pulled into my driveway one morning, got out of her car and screamed, "My water broke and this baby is coming now!" Let me say that my husband drove our car right down the median strip of Belmont Avenue with the horn blaring! When she planted her feet on the dashboard I thought he would have a heart attack! "Oh no you don't push!" I screamed. We flew into Northside OB parking lot on two wheels and thank God the nurse came running with the wheelchair. Her words, "This one came in on a wing and a prayer, don't worry sweetie we are almost there." I never forgot those words and her daughter came into this world three minutes later, on a wing and a prayer.

It troubles me when I hear another say, "If that person would have had more faith, God would have healed him." This is a very misguided and damaging statement. It can cause Christians to be disheartened and maybe even falter. We have all experienced the loss of a loved one. Does this mean we didn't pray enough? Believe enough? Trust enough? Dear God in heaven, how could anyone hold these thoughts in their mind and worse yet express them to one who is grieving? One of the most memorable stories in the Bible is when Jesus raised Lazarus from the dead! But guess what guys? Lazarus still died! He eventually died as we all will. Our bodies were knit together in our mother's womb. God planned it, and He knew us before we were ever born. There is a time for every season; a time to live and a time to die. Well surely believing and asking God for help can bring healing. I believe this is absolutely true, but when God calls you home, it has nothing to do with how strong your faith is. It is simply your appointed time to rejoice with your Father in heaven. I don't know why some join Him at such a young age, but you can be sure that God knows. Someone, somewhere, somehow was touched by God when these sorrows came to be. I know this because I have experienced it firsthand when my mom died. Most of my friends know that I found her body. She was too young, too wonderful, and too precious to die. It took me one year to accept why; not exactly why, but to find peace. Her death caused me to ask Jesus Christ into my life. Romans 8:28 "All things work together for the good for those who are called according to His purpose." Before my mom died I had no purpose in my life with God, but through this tragic loss came peace, knowledge, and joy. When you find yourself so low, there is only one place to go. I lifted my eyes to God, cried out to Him and mercifully He took me in. My mom died; as a matter of fact, my entire family, parents, brothers have all passed away. I see life as a gift, but life with God is indescribable. When I go from here to "There" well, I'll leave my loved ones behind in prayer. A prayer that is answered in God's way. For all of us, all of us will pass away. Thank God it has nothing to do with what we believe. That is the devil's desire to deceive. Our faith is more than a Bible story. It is going to eternal life to live in glory. So, your faith, my faith does not hold us here. It is a Divine appointment when God draws us near. Prayer is truly essential and He loves to hear us pray. But our faith, belief, and prayers, though grand, will not alter the celebration He has planned. It was never about faith or fate. Only God knows the time and date. When at last we see His face, there will be no thought of the previous place. Faith is how we live each day and it pulls us closer when we pray. One more breath He gives to me. Till one day a final sigh, for this old body was meant to die, but the spirit was meant to fly to the heavens on your prayer. On an eagle's wing without a care; to be with God my Father, who waits there...

Feeling a fluttering, warmth
That brings His holy sigh
I am there with my Father
Left behind loved ones to cry.

I rode your prayer to heaven
Please do not wonder why
There is peace, so much peace
It was time for me to die.

Do not ponder your faith
Believing we could rearrange
For my God the Father knows
Some things prayers won't change.

There is a celebration, grand!
The angels are singing my story
I rode your prayer to heaven
To my Father to share His Glory.

Do not ponder your belief
The date was divinely appointed
He waits patiently for each of us
By Him we are all anointed.

Feeling a fluttering, warmth
As His presence fills the air
Riding on an eagle's wing, to
Heaven: On a wing and a prayer.

Proverbs 23:5
"They fly away like an eagle toward heaven."

Exodus 19:4
**"Have you seen what I did to the Egyptians, and how I
bore you on eagle's wings and brought you to Myself."**

Day 7– by Stephanie M. White

Isaiah 57:1 NIV
The righteous perish, and no one ponders it in his heart;
devout men are taken away, and no one understands
that the righteous are taken away to be spared from
evil.

As we ponder death, we must remember this verse. God is merciful. Many times we do not understand God's plan or His timing, but this verse shows us that His plan is for our ultimate good.

We have no idea what our loved ones are being spared from by being taken home. Life is full of hurts and pain; some pains are never recovered from. Every pain can find recovery in Christ, but there are times when people cannot find their way to that recovery. God may have been sparing your loved one from just such a pain.

We must especially remember the love that God has for us during these times. God is love; He is not hate, anger, or punishment. He has *not* taken your loved one away from you for vindictive or vile reasons. We can find comfort knowing that God is lovingly directing our lives.

This passing of our loved one is a painful time for us, but it is precious in God's sight. It is a valuable, prized, and beloved time.

Psalms 116:15 NIV Precious in the sight of the LORD is the death of His saints.

The death of a child of God is precious in God's sight. It is the time for God to be united with His child in eternity. What a wonderful union and time of rejoicing. The culmination of our life here on earth is the beginning of our eternal love story. The love of God envelops His child as He brings them home to spend eternity with Him. If we could only see what they are seeing now, we would long to be where they are rather than have them back where we are!

Rejoice in the Lord
Do not be anxious or fear
Let your gentleness be evident
Rejoice, for the Lord is near.

Rejoice in the Lord
Pray with complete thanksgiving
His peace will guard your heart
Your life will be worth living.

Rejoice in the Lord
Embrace what is noble and true
Petitions will be answered
He desires to give this to you.

Rejoice in the Lord
Remain close, admirable and pure
His peace transcends all understanding
There is nothing you cannot endure.

Rejoice in the Lord
For He is loving and kind
Everything you will ever learn
In Jesus Christ, you will find.

Rejoice in the Lord
Even when you are broken
The love of God will strengthen
Just receive the words spoken.

Rejoice in the Lord
Your troubles you may plead
Rejoice, rejoice, rejoice
He will meet your every need.

Philippians 4:4-9

Day 9 – by Stephanie M. White

Psalms 10:14 NIV
But You, O God, do see trouble and grief; You consider it to take it in hand. The victim commits himself to You; You are the helper of the fatherless.

As a victim of grief we must commit ourselves to God. A victim is a person who is hurt or harmed by something or someone. Loss hurts; loss can harm. Loss can trouble us and leave us in a place of sorrow and heartache. Our anguish will never see its end if we refuse to commit ourselves to the Lord.

Committing ourselves to the Lord involves entrusting Him with our pain, handing our unanswered questions over to Him, and assigning ourselves to His care. Entrusting God with your pain is simply being honest with Him. He knows how you are hurting. He longs to comfort you, but that comfort will escape us if we are not honest about our feelings. Some try to disguise grief; some try to avoid it. We need to know that our pain does not make us faithless or less of a Christian. Pain is a normal emotion. We can entrust Him with our pain.

We must also be willing to live without all of the answers we may like to have. Living by faith is living by every word that proceeds from the mouth of God; sometimes, we must be content with God's Divine plan even when we do not understand it. The Word will comfort us as we abide in it and those questions will become less essential as faith takes over.

As you are mourning, you must assign yourself to His care. Assigning yourself to His care is nothing more than abiding in His Word. When we assign ourselves to someone's care in the natural, we are placing ourselves in their hands. We are lodging where they lodge; we are depending on them. As we abide in the Word of God we will begin to depend more and more on Christ; this is the key to the transformation from victim to victor. Place yourself in His care; abide in His Word!

Our God longs to comfort us. He longs to help us; however, we must receive what He is offering. Let God help you; commit yourself to His care.

Day 10 – by Kathleen Higham
The Only Son

"There are no words," I said
Reaching out to wipe her tear
A stranger I had never met
Yet God would draw us near.

"I lost my son, my only son"
In her brokenness came a plead
We shared the intimacy of grief
And the heart of a woman's creed.

For only a mother can understand
The sorrow of the ultimate pain
A trial comes so unspeakable
As the fires pour down like rain.

"Oh my God," she cries out!
My son was everything that mattered
Now a heart beats cold and empty
Her world was completely shattered.

The sun may shine, not for her
Relentlessly, time passes even still
When a memory plagues her soul
Of a man dragging a cross up a hill.

"I lost my son, my only son"
In the despair of that night
But the mother of God before me
Knew, that agony brings the light.

The Son of God, the only Son
Who was crucified to fill our need
So a dark and void heart could speak
The words of a mother's creed.

"Oh my God," she cries out!
You're work in me is never done
To perpetuate forever, a woman's creed
For our Lord and Savior, the only Son.

Jeremiah 17:14 AMP
**Heal me, O Lord, and I shall be healed; save me, and I
shall be saved, for You are my praise.**

Many times grief is accompanied by a feeling of disappointment. We hear of God's promises for healing; and yet, we have lost a loved one. Does this mean that God ignored our prayer? Did we not have enough faith? Is God's Word only true for some? Am I not loved by God like those who experience the miracle in this life?

These questions, and more, enter our minds during a time of grieving and we must make sure we answer them and understand the Word. God is love; His love for us is the same as His love for another. His promises are not received by those He "favors" over another. Healing is His promise, and healing *is* received – there are just some cases where it is received in *this* life. Death is promised to all; however, with death comes the ultimate healing. Death is eternal healing. As we enter God's eternal presence we receive a new body that will never be sick or experience pain. God's promise of healing was not broken because our loved one died; it was received completely.

Our loved one did not die because we were ignored by God. They did not die because we did not have enough faith. They did not die because God's Word is not true. They did not die because God did not love you enough to heal them. We must reject these false ideas about death and understand the truth. Your loved one passed on from this life because death passes upon all men (Romans 5:12). We may not understand the timing, but we can rest assured that our times are in His hands (Psalms 31:15) and that His timing is perfect.

As we contemplate our faith during a time of grief we must understand that faith is the result of abiding in the Word. If we feel that our faith is lacking, we can know that we need more of His Word. Press past the pain of grief and bask in His Word. His Word will heal your pain; it is the answer you are seeking. In your grief, you can still praise God for the perfectly complete healing your loved one is experiencing now!

Day 12 – by Kathleen Higham
Just By Chance

Nothing is ever just by chance
That an old friend I would see
Two hearts collide with memories
As she shares her thoughts with me.

Nothing is ever just by chance
I hear her passion, her sorrow
A Mother hanging on to life
A daughter praying for tomorrow.

Nothing is ever just by chance
When tender words are spoken
An amazing family I visualize
Knowing their hearts will be broken.

Nothing is ever just by chance
Writing of this encounter, Divine
Words from God will comfort her
As always He gives a sign.

Nothing is ever just by chance
Not one day will pass by
Thoughts of Mother embrace me
Then I breathe a heavy sigh.

Nothing is ever just by chance
He plans it from the start
His words flow to the paper
Words from this burdened heart.

Nothing is ever just by chance
I accept this gift He will give
Touching souls as tears fall down
This is the life that I live.

Nothing is ever just by chance
One day we all shall meet
Where the Mothers gather joyfully
In Glory at Jesus' feet.

Day 13 – by Stephanie M. White

Hebrews 2:14-15 AMP
Since, therefore, [these His] children share in flesh and blood [in the physical nature of human beings], He [Himself] in a similar manner partook of the same [nature], that by [going through] death He might bring to naught and make of no effect him who had the power of death--that is, the devil--And also that He might deliver and completely set free all those who through the [haunting] fear of death were held in bondage throughout the whole course of their lives.

Death. To many it is an adversary. To the Christian, it is a victory. The fear of death is a very common phobia. As Christians, we do not have to fear death. Sure, we may fear *how* death may come, but death itself has been overcome. Even when fearing how death may come, we can be comforted by the story of Stephen in the Bible (Acts 7). Stephen was actually praying for others as death was approaching. I believe that God comforts us even in the most violent of deaths. My son took a class in college and he was sharing with me what he learned regarding death. He told me that certain chemicals are released when a person is dying and these chemicals have a pain relieving effect. God's amazing love for us planned ahead for the pain some would suffer; what an amazing God! We can trust God with our lives and even with our death.

Death has been overcome! The process by which we leave this temporary world and enter our eternal home is nothing more than a transition. We do not have to fear death when we know the One who overcame death for us. Death is not the end for those who know Christ. Death is the closing of one chapter in life and the opening of the eternal novel God is writing about us. Death is not to be feared; death is to be anticipated with joy because we will be with our faithful Lover.

As we grieve for a loved one, it is important for us to bear in mind that there is nothing to fear; Jesus Christ has overcome death and we can look forward to eternal life!

Day 14 – by Kathleen Higham
A Hundred Fingers

Her beauty comes to greet me
My eyes recognize that smile
Memories of a burdened past
She will walk with me awhile.

Marveling at a sculptured face
For age has touched her not
Then words flow so gracefully
Once more, wisdom I've sought.

She reveals to me a sorrow
Of a Mother who is ill
And a family pulls together
They will care for her until.

I imagine this amazing woman
As a hundred fingers caress
Ten children caring for a Mom
For her there can be no less.

Stunned by this personal encounter
Where one soul touches another
I pray for a peaceful passing
Understanding the love of a Mother.

I am mesmerized by their numbers
Hearts committed, every last one
Twenty hands, a hundred fingers
Until her life on earth is done.

A love story of their faithfulness
A Mother will be sadly missed
Twenty hands, a hundred fingers
Each one she lovingly kissed.

Proverbs 31:29

Day 15 – by Stephanie M. White

Isaiah 25:8 MSG
Yes, He'll banish death forever. And GOD will wipe the tears from every face. He'll remove every sign of disgrace from His people, wherever they are. Yes! GOD says so!

We can be sure that death is not our enemy! We can be sure that death will not triumph over us or our loved ones in Christ!

This sadness that we feel as a result of a loss in this life is only temporary. God has an amazing future planned for His children and death is not a part of it!

Death can be defined as the end of life; however, God's definition of death is somewhat different.

> 2 Corinthians 5:8 KJV We are confident, [I say], and willing rather to be absent from the body, and to be present with the Lord.

God defines death as the beginning of eternity in His presence. No wonder there will be no more tears!

We must be confident of this truth. We must walk in faith regarding death. We can only do this if we are abiding in His Word. The Word shows us the truth regarding death; it opens our eyes to the beauty of a life that is spent with the Lord. Grief can find comfort in God's promises. As you abide in the Word on heaven you will find yourself at peace. Knowing that your loved one is in the arms of Jesus brings a peace that eludes the unsaved. While it does not bring back your loved one, it does give you the confirmation of a reunion in the future. If we can understand that this separation is only temporary, we can joyfully look forward to the future. This does not mean that we will never feel sadness regarding this temporary loss, but it does mean that we can endure and see victory in spite of the feelings grief produces!

Hold on to the promises of God and never forget that you *will* see your loved ones again – Yes! God says so!

Day 16 – by Kathleen Higham
A Precious Boy

He truly was a precious boy
A boy who learned to love
When to his Mother, a kiss
A kiss sent from God above.

It seems it was his first kiss
A Mother prayed for years
A glimpse into his Godly heart
This gift bore many tears.

The first kiss, but not the last
God took him by the hand
A tiny soul went to Heaven
So hard to imagine, understand.

He truly was a precious boy
As one by one friends spoke
Of a child who loved Jesus
Hearts cried, then voices broke.

Though his life was very short
His passing brings a tender story
Many hands raised to the Lord
Surrendering their lives to Glory.

The loss was surely devastating
Yet, there is an inexplicable joy
When souls will go to Heaven
Just because of this little boy.

The first kiss, a new beginning
Lending time for hearts to mend
While a precious boy in Heaven
Gives his kisses without end.

Day 17 – by Stephanie M. White

Psalms 31:9-10 NIV
Be merciful to me, O LORD, for I am in distress; my eyes grow weak with sorrow, my soul and my body with grief. My life is consumed by anguish and my years by groaning; my strength fails because of my affliction, and my bones grow weak.

There will be days when the agony we feel will seem to get the better of us. When you encounter days such as these remind yourself of the mercy of the Lord.

The Lord your God longs to show you mercy. He is willing to reach out and meet your need, but you must receive. During the worst days of mourning you may not feel like receiving – you may not feel like abiding in the Word. That is okay; your feelings are normal, but you still must overcome those feelings. Even though you may not feel like reading you can still listen to the Bible on CD or you can listen to praise music or a message. Find a way to take the Word in no matter how you feel.

Distress can overwhelm us; the Word is our weapon against this devastation. Lives are consumed by grief when the Word is disregarded. We can forfeit the future God has for us by ignoring His Word.

Suffering loss is not something to be minimized; it is not something we can make light of, but it does not have to be the end for us. God wants to see us through this time and take us to what He has in store. Bear in mind that ultimately you will be reunited with the ones you are missing.

2 Corinthians 4:17 NIV For our light and momentary troubles are achieving for us an eternal glory that far outweighs them all.

On our worst days we would do well to remind ourselves that this is only temporary! The struggle you are enduring will result in an eternal glory that will far outweigh it!

Day 18 – by Kathleen Higham
A Tear Away

She is just a tear away
As I bring her to my mind
The one who carried me inside
In my heart I'll always find.

She is just a tear away
Of this I am absolutely sure
Astonished by her courage
My life is defined by her.

She is just a tear away
Yet I see her every day
Hard to imagine all these years
But because of her I pray.

She is just a tear away
Oh how much I've cried
My God promises I'll see her
Didn't know that when she died.

She is just a tear away
And every decision I make
I think about what God would do
Believing He would never forsake.

She is just a tear away
For time is of no essence
She will hold me close again
With the Lord in our presence.

She is just a tear away
A tear falling to its end
I will be with her once more
My Mom, my truest friend.

Isaiah 61:1-3 NIV
The Spirit of the Sovereign LORD is on Me, because the
LORD has anointed Me to preach good news to the poor.
He has sent Me to bind up the brokenhearted, to
proclaim freedom for the captives and release from
darkness for the prisoners, to proclaim the year of the
Lord's favor and the day of vengeance of our God, to
comfort all who mourn, and provide for those who
grieve in Zion-- to bestow on them a crown of beauty
instead of ashes, the oil of gladness instead of
mourning, and a garment of praise instead of a spirit of
despair. They will be called oaks of righteousness, a
planting of the LORD for the display of His splendor.

You were created to display His splendor! Your loving Father
wants to see you through this time of mourning and take you
into a place of comfort and joy. This may seem impossible
right now as you grieve, but the impossible *is* possible with
God! Your bad days do not determine your future.

I am not saying that you will cease to miss your loved
one, but I am saying that God can heal your broken heart.
Right now you may feel like a prisoner of grief, but God has
other plans. Grief does not have to control you when you
abide in the Word and let His love see you through. Faith and
patience bring about every one of God's promises (Hebrews
6:12); patience is that season of grief in this instance. It will
take time.

As I miss loved ones, I am comforted *knowing* that I *will*
see them again. Thinking of eternity with my loved ones
always brings joy. I lost a grandmother who always hosted
Christmas Eve at her home. This celebration is now at my
home, but it has never been the same. I look forward to
celebrating with her again in eternity! Christmas may never be
the same, but I can still enjoy the celebration because I can
look ahead to what God has planned for us in eternity! Share
your glimpse of eternity and display God's splendor!

I dreamed the last dance in my heart
From the echoes of a song I shall depart
Not to leave my loved ones here to cry
I am singing joyfully up on high.

I dreamed the first dance with my true love
The Father God my Savior from above
From the echoes of the song I sing anew
The last dance now begins my life with You.

The last dance now remembered on this earth
But His music called to me from my birth
The gifts that I have shared for all these years
May bring to some a melody of tears.

I dreamed the last dance in my heart
As God had choreographed it from the start
Look to the heavens though it may seem far
See me dance the last dance on a star.

Singing for the one that I adored
My voice lifts up in praise to my Lord
The last dance thru the glory of heaven's door
I dance at last with Him forevermore...

In memory of Donna Summer

Day 21 – by Stephanie M. White

Psalms 30:11-12 NLT
You have turned my mourning into joyful dancing. You have taken away my clothes of mourning and clothed me with joy, that I might sing praises to You and not be silent. O LORD my God, I will give You thanks forever!

Only God can turn our mourning into joy; this is a Spiritual process. Our flesh cannot experience joy; joy is a fruit of the Spirit and every fruit of the Spirit is produced the same way – by consistently abiding in the Word of God.

God understands our feelings. He understands death; He experienced the death of His Son. We can rest assured that He also knows how to bring us through. Second Peter, chapter one and verse three, tells us that God has given us everything we need for life – life includes mourning. God has provided us with the Spiritual weapon of His Word. We cannot be reminded enough of the importance of the Word. His Word can defeat the overwhelming effect that grief can have on us.

How can we dance when we are mourning? We can dance by faith. We can dance because we know that we will see our loved ones again. Joyful dancing is the result of knowing God's promises and living by faith regarding those promises. Faith comes from hearing the Word (Romans 10:17); this "hearing" is a *continual* intake of the Word. The more we fill ourselves with the Word, the more we will experience joy in spite of the circumstances.

As we think about joy during a time of grief we may feel guilty for even considering dancing again. This guilt is not from God. This victory over mourning does not mean that we no longer miss our loved ones. It simply means that we are going to embrace this life because we understand the brevity of it. We recognize the impact our loved one had on us and through Christ we want to see our lives impact others.

If we could speak to those we've lost, they would surely tell us to embrace life. They would tell us that they love to see us happy and full of joy. Your loved one would not be angry with you because you are dancing; they would be delighted!

Day 22 – by Kathleen Higham
Grains Of Sand

It's hard to understand this Lord
For a son and a brother went to sleep
Our hearts are heavy with sorrow
But he wasn't ours to keep.

This life that You have given us
Is of endless grains of sand
And our life is pouring from them
As each grain sifts through Your Hand.

For we will never ever know
When the final grain will fall
Timeless hands will lift us up
On that day You come to call.

The one who is sitting at Your feet
He was my brother and my friend
But Lord I wasn't ready
For my brother's life to end.

Now I am weeping on my knees
And my family reaches out to You
As the grains of sand are pouring down
But You promised to see us through.

For we know You have an awesome plan
And grains of sand are just a number
Your Hand has been the sifter
The Father wakes us from our slumber.

And never again will we fall asleep
Life everlasting is Your gift
Forever we will live with You
When there is no more sand to sift.

Day 23 – by Stephanie M. White

1 Corinthians 7:31 NLT
Those who use the things of the world should not become attached to them. For this world as we know it will soon pass away.

Grief can teach us many things; one is the succinctness of this life. Learn from those who have gone on ahead of you. As you remember your loved ones remember what is really important.

This world is temporary; it is transitory. This world is not our home. We are not to pretend that this life is meaningless; we are to simply live this life according to the next. There are some who do not plan or take care of things here and they use eternity as an excuse for their indolence. God is not asking us to ignore the present; in fact, He tells us to live each day to the full! He tells us to work, to take care of our families, to celebrate, and so on. God is a lover of life and God wants us to love our life here, too!

> 1 Timothy 6:17 NIV Command those who are rich in this present world...to put their hope in God, who richly provides us with everything for our enjoyment.

Whatever God has given you is to be enjoyed, but it is to be enjoyed realizing that it is only temporary. As we grieve a loss we can see this brevity of life. No one can take their belongings with them, but we do take everything that was done through Christ with us! For example, we cannot take our paycheck with us, but we can take work that was done through Christ. God cares about the origination of our actions (1 Corinthians 3:13). What is done in the flesh is fleeting. Only what is done by faith will last. This means that we are to abide in the Word concerning the every-day. Parent through the Word, work through the Word, enjoy your marriage through the Word, grieve through the Word and so on. Stay cognizant of the fact that anything done in the flesh will pass away. Learn from those who have gone on ahead of us. Their life can influence yours when you do and their legacy can live on!

Day 24 – by Kathleen Higham
God's Promise

I've lost my friend my true love
It feels still and quiet here
He was everything that mattered
My heart is filled with fear.

Early mornings when I awake
Reaching out to feel his touch
Remembering with shocking pain
And I miss him oh so much.

How can I live without this man
With whom I've spent my life
For he was sweet and gentle
And God let me be his wife.

Looking back I marvel
At this man who protected me
I close my eyes and wish for him
But his face I cannot see.

And many nights I cry aloud
God what have you done
It's dark and lonely lying here
As I'm waiting for the sun.

When morning comes a heavy sigh
Lord give me strength today
Lift me up remembering
My husband has gone away.

Touch my broken shattered heart
Until You come for me
And bring me to the man I love
As You promised forever we'll be.

Day 25 – by Stephanie M. White

Psalms 6:3-4 NLT
I am sick at heart. How long, O LORD, until You restore me? Return, O LORD, and rescue me. Save me because of Your unfailing love.

As we go through a period of grieving we may often times wonder how much longer we can go on feeling this way. When our heart aches and we are in anguish, we feel weak. Weakness can only last for so long until a person is overcome.

As we struggle with the heartbreak that bereavement can bring, we must be sure to focus on the Lord and His unfailing love. We must never believe that God took a loved one for any other reason than His love. There are some who feel like God allowed death to take place because He was angry or He was inflicting punishment. This is not true. Remember that the death of one of God's children is precious in His sight and death is the beginning of their eternal walk with God. Death is not a negative event in the Spiritual; it is a celebration. We do not always feel like this is the truth, but it is. Our loss here is heaven's gain. We have to bear in mind that our loved ones in Christ are in a miraculous home with our Lord. We are the ones who are feeling the pain; they are not. We must find a way to outlast the pain that death can bring – and there is only one way to do this; it is abiding in the Word of God!

The Word of God reminds us continually of God's love for us. It paints a picture of our new home in heaven. It reminds us that this home on earth is temporary. The Word is the only thing that can help us grieve Spiritually and move on to what God has for us despite our loss.

We will never forget the loved ones who are no longer with us here, but we can look forward to seeing them again because of God's unfailing love. Open your heart to His comfort and His promises. His love for you has provided you with an eternal home in heaven; you will be with Him and your loved ones one day soon. His love for you can rescue you from a life of grieving if you allow it.

Day 26 – by Kathleen Higham
Grief

No one ever leaves this world
Without feeling grief's wrath
There are no words to express
Why some travel this hurtful path.

Yet each of us will experience
A loss that cuts so deep
An overwhelming helplessness
When awakened from our sleep.

There can be no understanding
But the Lord feels our despair
Relentlessly He walks with us
Every moment He is there.

There are times when succumbing
Would bring some relief
But, wherein lies the answer?
To surviving this endless grief.

Only time will heal a heart
That breaks with every tear
Then grief will slowly leave you
And God will draw you near.

Still, the pain may be distant
Remembering with a nagging fear
About the loved one who left us
His voice we no longer hear.

Begging for just one dream
As you sorrow into the night
Yet, the very cross that burdens
Will carry you through the fight.

No one ever leaves this world
It seems we all must grieve
No one ever leaves this world, but
In God's promise, I do believe.

Matthew 5:4
"Blessed are those who mourn, For they shall be comforted."

Job 5:8-11 AMP
As for me, I would seek God and inquire of and require Him, and to God would I commit my cause-- Who does great things and unsearchable, marvelous things without number, Who gives rain upon the earth and sends waters upon the fields, so that He sets on high those who are lowly, and those who mourn He lifts to safety.

Have you committed your cause to God? Have you given Him the grief that you are not supposed to bear?

Grief is not something we *can* bear; we need God! God can take the pain and agony that we are feeling and He can do great things!

I have witnessed funeral after funeral that resulted in lives being given to Christ. What a marvelous thing! My dad is a Pastor and he never closes a funeral without giving the listeners the Word of God. He explains that Jesus Christ took our place and paid the price for our sin. So many have never heard the plan of God's salvation before. They may never enter a church for any other reason than a funeral.

Mourning can lift us to safety if we seek Christ. For some, they are introduced to Christ as the result of a death; for others, they are reintroduced to Christ. Christ is uniquely revealed to us when we suffer loss; we may have known Him for years, but when we suffer loss He reveals Himself to us in a way that only a mourner could appreciate. No matter what category you fall in, you must remember that only Christ can take you from mourning to a place of safety. Mourning can turn into a dangerous state if we do not commit that grief to Christ.

Grief that is left unchecked can lead us into many precarious situations. It can lead to depression, withdrawal, anxiety, and more. Do not try to grieve alone; invite Christ into your situation. Only He can comfort you and enable you to press on to the future.

Day 28 – by Kathleen Higham
Heaven Holds Many of Mine

Life can surely be exquisite
If you breathe, breathe Him in
Peace, peace unfathomable comes
No room, no room for sin.

Surrendering every single thought
The Holy Spirit will draw near
Then fill you so completely
Conquering every imagined fear.

But one, a fear of mortals
That brings a heartfelt sigh
When God comes to claim one
Tears fall down as we cry.

The most pondered question comes
Why did my loved one have to die?
Knowing Heaven opens the door
Still, there is the thought, why?

Heaven holds many of mine
Thoughts of them fill my head
But I know, I know I am going
For this is what God said.

"I will never forsake you"
To Christians He gives a sign
Let Me come inside your heart
Then forever you are Mine.

Heaven holds many of mine
Someday my loved ones I'll see
For His promise is eternal life
With Him exalted and free.

1 Thessalonians 4:13

Day 29 – by Stephanie M. White

Hosea 13:14 NIV
I will ransom them from the power of the grave; I will redeem them from death. Where, O death, are your plagues? Where, O grave, is your destruction?...

Through Christ we have been ransomed from the power of the grave!

The Hebrew word translated as "ransom" means to sever, to release, to rescue, and to liberate. God is declaring our liberation from the power of the grave. He has severed the power it had over us. What is the power of the grave?

There are several things that can be listed as the "power of the grave." For some, the power of the grave is fear. Fear can be erased when we understand what Christ has done for us. We no longer will fear death when we see it as the beginning of life in heaven. We will not incessantly fear the loss of others when we know that we will be reunited with them in paradise. Fear is eradicated as Godly wisdom is received through His Word.

The word translated as "power" is the Hebrew word "yad" and part of its definition is "fellowship." For some, fellowshipping with death is customary. This can include living in the past, constantly thinking about death, and living in fear of death.

Sometimes we can be stationary in grief. Instead of moving forward, we can let life pass us by because we never look to God during the natural grieving process.

Some people live in phobic states as a result of an irrational death mentality. Death is part of this life. Death is not an enemy; it is not to be feared. We are not to be preoccupied with it. Death is the end of this life and the beginning of eternity. It should be looked forward to, seeing that it ushers us into eternity with Christ, but it should not be consuming our thoughts in a negative way.

Look to the Word of God for the truth on death and you, too, can live ransomed from its power!

Day 30 – by Kathleen Higham
Her Silky Wings

Pondering the sight of Heaven
Instilled because of this child
Thoughts of her touch me
Becoming completely beguiled.

Aware of the existence of angels
They tended to her with such care
As they gently took her to Heaven
The Lord was waiting for her there.

Oh, the sweetness of His touch
His kisses covered her face
Silky wings He made for her
In Heaven, an unimaginable place.

Her life fulfilled in constant joy
Knowing they will come someday
Remembering hearts that beat as one
Even when she left that day.

The time they shared, a precious gift
But God had loved her more
Now she waits in hopefulness
By the gate, at Heaven's door.

Sometimes they will feel her
A whisper of her silky wing
So softly brushes by their lips
In that moment, the angels sing.

Life will pass very quickly
And her parents will finally know
Her silky wings come to guide them
When it is time for them to go.

John 16:20 NIV
I tell you the truth, you will weep and mourn while the world rejoices. You will grieve, but your grief will turn to joy.

Jesus speaks of His upcoming crucifixion and His disciples begin to experience grief. The thought of losing Him brought misery to their hearts. Jesus knew they would feel loss. He also knows that we feel loss; it is a normal human emotion – an emotion that *He* gave us. He did not rebuke them for this feeling; He encouraged them.

We can also be encouraged. Our grief will end in joy! There will come a day when we will be united with our loved ones and what a wonderful day that will be!

Just as the death of Jesus would bring life to us, the death of our loved ones in Christ results in life. As a child of God dies in this life, they are opening their eyes in their eternal home. They are exchanging their temporary, destructible body for a permanent, imperishable one! Their death is truly a beginning, not an ending.

We must understand that the death of our loved one is only a temporary separation from us. As a child of God we have a home in heaven to look forward to; we have been promised eternity in God's presence. We can look forward to a reunion that will never end!

Even though we experience grief here, we can look forward to a home in eternity where we will never experience it again! We will live a life of joy in heaven!

Revelation 21:4 KJV And God shall wipe away all tears from their eyes; and there shall be no more death, neither sorrow, nor crying, neither shall there be any more pain: for the former things are passed away.

This time of grieving is temporary. It may not seem like it now; but believe God, it is!

Day 32 – Kathleen Higham
His Hand

There are times I wonder
As I kneel to Him in prayer
My heart is filled with anguish
And I'm asking "Do You care?"

Are You standing by me
In a brilliant ray of light
Is Your hand upon me
As You pray with me tonight?

For there are oh so many
Whose pain is hard to bear
But when we seek our Father
The pain is His to share.

Never will a moment pass
That He is not aware
And He will groan to intercede
As He listens to our prayer.

But often we're impatient
And we find it hard to wait
But our Father's hand is on us
As He guides us to our fate.

For even as we wonder
Our Lord had wondered too
He begged His Holy Father
And His Father saw Him through.

So remember when we suffer
Our Father tells His Son
And the hand of Jesus touches us
Until our life on earth is done.

Day 33 – by Stephanie M. White

Psalms 25:15-17 NIV
My eyes are ever on the LORD, for only He will release my feet from the snare. Turn to me and be gracious to me, for I am lonely and afflicted. The troubles of my heart have multiplied; free me from my anguish.

Where is your focus during this season of grief? Your eyes need to be on the Lord! He alone can lead you out of grief and into joy.

"Only He will release my feet from the snare." Only God can set you free from the trap that the enemy tries to ensnare you in. The trap of grief is *remaining* in grief; it is never moving forward and enjoying life again. The combination of grief and guilt can prevent our enjoyment of life after we suffer a loss. If you battle with guilt, be assured that your loved one delights in your joy! They would never want to see you trapped in a perpetual state of grief.

We may feel lonely as a result of the death of a loved one, but remember that God has promised to never leave us.

Hebrews 13:5 NIV ...God has said, "Never will I leave you; never will I forsake you."

Even though we have suffered loss, we can be sure that God is by our side. We can also be sure that one day He will repeal that loss; one day we will join our loved ones never to part again.

The Psalmist is feeling lonely and he is asking God to turn to him. He feels as if God's face is turned away, but our feelings are not fact. The fact is that God's Word proves that God never leaves us. When we feel lonely we need to acknowledge His presence. Speak His promise to never leave you! If we are ever going to be set free from the anguish that loss can produce, we are going to have to turn our focus to the Word of God! Keep your focus on the Lord; keep your thoughts centered on the Word.

Day 34 – by Kathleen Higham
Hold Me

A precious friend confided in me that one night she felt filled with despair. She lay in her bed unable to say or do anything, but in that moment she whispered to God, "Please Hold Me." Then my friend tells me that a white light filled the air and she could feel Him holding her. Oh, if only we could ask Him knowing and believing that He would... (Isaiah 41:11)

Tonight I lay weary in my bed
A heavy sorrow fills my head
I do not want to feel this way
There are no words that I can say.

Still and rigid my eyes shut tight
No sleep will come on this night
The silence in a heart of dread
My body weighted down like lead.

I would cry, but I simply cannot
A losing battle if I had fought
Then I felt Him, could it be?
From my lips I say, "Hold me."

God hold me, hold me please
Unable to fall upon my knees
It hurts too much to even try
But the white light came to defy.

He held me with the softest sigh
And for just a moment I did cry
Understanding this to be a test
Now in His arms at last, I rest.

So ask Him in a that time of need
From every burden you are freed
If only you can say, "Hold me"
He would, just ask, ask and see.

Job 2:11-13 NIV

When Job's three friends, Eliphaz the Temanite, Bildad the Shuhite and Zophar the Naamathite, heard about all the troubles that had come upon him, they set out from their homes and met together by agreement to go and sympathize with him and comfort him. When they saw him from a distance, they could hardly recognize him; they began to weep aloud, and they tore their robes and sprinkled dust on their heads. Then they sat on the ground with him for seven days and seven nights. No one said a word to him, because they saw how great his suffering was.

A season of grief can open our eyes to the suffering of others. When we experience grief, we then can easily relate with others who are suffering in the same way.

This passage in Job is a favorite of mine. We should all desire to be this kind of friend. A friend who will put their life on hold just to sit with another friend.

At first, these friends didn't say a word. Grief is not an occasion for countless words. There are times when it is hard to speak because we are experiencing a loss. We do not always have to have the perfect words for every occasion; many times a person just wants a hug or simply to know that you care.

These friends tore their robes and wept *with* their friend.

Romans 12:15 NIV Rejoice with those who rejoice; mourn with those who mourn.

Feeling the pain of another is a Spiritual action; it is the result of abiding in the Word. We cannot mourn with those who mourn if we are walking in the flesh. The flesh thinks only of itself. If you have a friend who is mourning with you, thank *God* for them!   When your season of grief has passed you may have the opportunity to do the same for them.

Day 36 – by Kathleen Higham
Misery Loves Company

Life can be so painful
But help is on the way
God will surely carry you
As He waits for you to pray.

For it is just a simple truth
When we are suffering in fear
No one wants to be alone
So prayer draws others near.

And misery loves company
We eagerly share our grief
Knowing those around us
Bring peace and some relief.

But only God can save us
Calling us by two or more
Come, come and pray to Me
I stand here at your door.

So we gather together in hope
Speaking to Him with one voice
Knowing He hears each separately
Then in Him our souls rejoice.

Yes misery loves company
But it will take its leave
Where two or more are gathered
Then to God we'll cleave.

Remember the company we keep
Are Christians oh so dear
Holding hands in heartfelt prayer
And the misery will disappear.

Matthew 18:20

Psalms 10:17 NIV
You hear, O LORD, the desire of the afflicted; You
encourage them, and You listen to their cry.

You may be mourning alone. You may not have a friend that will mourn with you, but there is a Friend that sticks closer than a brother (Proverbs 18:24)!

Even when no one else is around, we always have the privilege of going to God. God is never too tired or too busy to listen. God is available to us at any time. How many times do we ignore the Friend that sticks closer than anyone else ever will? God is willing to hear us; we must be willing to pray.

The desire of the afflicted is heard by God. He is attentive to our longings and He has an answer for every one of us. As we pour out our hearts in prayer, we must also look to His Word for the answers we desire. God is listening to us; we must listen to Him. We listen by hearing His Word.

> Jeremiah 23:18 NIV But which of them has stood in the council of the LORD to see or to hear His word? Who has listened and heard His word?

Are we hearing the Word? The word translated as "hear" is the Hebrew word "shama." This word means to hear intelligently, to (gather) together, consider, be content with, declare, show (forth), and understand. This word is often translated as "obey" also. Hearing the Word is not casual reading. Hearing involves gathering – it requires finding and collecting God's promises for your need. If you are a hearer of the Word you are content with the Word – you need no outside proof besides the promise of God. As you gather the Word and abide in it, the Word will show forth in your life.

The Word of God is His love letter to us; it is full of His promises for our lives. It is our source of encouragement. There is an answer in the Word for every question we will have in this life; we must seek it out and abide in it. Hold on to the promises of God; He is faithful to every one of them!

Day 38 – by Kathleen Higham
Jesus Suffered More

Having suffered endless pain
I lived the story well
But my Jesus suffered more
As He descended into hell.

Oh, death has surely grieved me
Left me searching, broken, bare
But my Jesus suffered more
Through all of it He was there.

I have committed the vilest sin
Even forgot that God existed
But my Jesus suffered more
When on the cross He persisted.

There have been spiritual battles
And far too many I have lost
But my Jesus suffered more
He paid the horrific cost.

Lovers came and misled me
Filled a lonely heart with desire
But my Jesus suffered more
Proved all of them the liar.

My body has been brutalized
I am sickened to the core
But my Jesus suffered more
Only God could survive, endure.

I have truly been forsaken
Not deserving in His sight
But my Jesus suffered more
He was crucified that night.

I have cried until exhausted
Could not stand upon my feet
But my Jesus suffered more
Then made my soul complete.

No tears, no sorrow, no crying
I will fall on bended knee
My Jesus suffered, suffered more
To give peace and life to me.

His life brings everlasting joy
As I walk through Heaven's door
The truth of all my sorrow speaks
That my Jesus suffered more.

Day 39 – by Stephanie M. White

Psalms 19:7-8 NIV
The law of the LORD is perfect, reviving the soul. The statutes of the LORD are trustworthy, making wise the simple. The precepts of the LORD are right, giving joy to the heart. The commands of the LORD are radiant, giving light to the eyes.

The Word of God is perfect; it is complete. It is everything we need for this life. The Word revives our soul. Our soul is our mind, our will, and our emotions. A season of grief affects the soul. Grief touches our mind, our will, and our emotions.

The mind is a controlling factor in life; what course our mind is on determines the course of our lives (Proverbs 23:7 KJV). When we grieve, our mind can wander towards the negative. Thoughts of depression, anger, fear, and so on, can monopolize the mind during a period of mourning. The Word of God is the perfect solution for a wandering mind. The Word of God will renew our minds *if* we remain in it.

Our will is also affected during a season of grief. Our will is a decision maker in our lives. Our will includes our determination and inclination. If we are not focused on the Word of God during a time of mourning, our decisions will not be Spiritually based. We may tend to fall in line with the grief rather than fight the grief with the Word of God. If we want our will to be in line with God's will, then we must focus on the Word of God. The Word changes our will; it gives us a proclivity for the things that agree with the Word.

Finally, and sometimes most obviously, our emotions are impacted during a season of grief. We will experience a variety of emotions during the grieving process. As these feelings fluctuate, we can minimize the control these emotions have over us by staying focused on the Word of God. Emotions that are left unchecked can have a negative impact on us and those around us.

As we go through the process of grieving, we must be sure to maintain our relationship with the Word.

Day 40 – by Kathleen Higham
Lily

I saw an angel today
On her tummy she lies
So delicate, yet perfect
Touched her with my eyes.

I am mesmerized by Lily
And this battle she has bore
When her tiny hand unfolds
God closes it once more.

I saw an angel today
In her my God speaks
If only I could hold her
Kiss those precious cheeks.

As I pray for mercy
Already His miracle here
A little heart beats furiously
Each breath brings another tear.

I saw an angel today
And when the alarms sound
Doctors and nurses come together
They work on hallowed ground.

I have felt His presence
Even technology cannot claim
The quiet peace that comes to me
As I say His Holy Name.

I saw two angels today
The one who loves her so
My daughter tenderly cares for her
The nurse who won't let go.

Matthew 19:14

Day 41 – by Stephanie M. White

Psalms 119:28 MSG
My sad life's dilapidated, a falling-down barn; build me up again by Your Word.

Your may feel as if you are falling to pieces during a season of grief, but you must know that continuing through this devotional is building you back up again! The Word of God is being planted and you are receiving exactly what you need to rebuild.

There will be more than one occasion in life where we feel broken down. As we experience such times, we must always know the method of rebuilding. Only the Word of God can build what has been torn down. Only the Word can bring life into what feels like death. You may have to receive the Word through tears, but receive it nonetheless! Press on in the Word. You may not even feel like you can read, but you can listen. Listen to the Word on CD or TV. Do whatever you have to do to be rebuilt. God's promise to you is restoration.

> Jeremiah 31:3-4 NIV The LORD appeared to us in the past, saying: "I have loved you with an everlasting love; I have drawn you with loving-kindness. I will build you up again and you will be rebuilt..."

The love of God can rebuild your life! I am not saying that your life will be better without your lost loved one; I am saying that it will be different, but it can be worth living again. Life is never truly the same after you suffer loss, but it is still worth living. As you begin to rebuild through the Word, remind yourself that this is a temporary separation! Look forward to the eternal reunion with your loved ones who have gone on ahead of you! Take hold of life and live it to the fullest; live it in honor of those who are no longer with us. Not one of our loved ones would want to see us living a life of decay. Honor their memory by embracing your life and making more memories of your own. One day this temporary separation will be no more!

Day 42 – by Kathleen Higham
Only Time

Time is passing so quickly
No longer standing still
At times a little fear creeps in
Thinking, I am over the hill.

The mirror is not my friend
And so often there is strife
It's not so easy anymore
I wonder about my life.

Time is passing so quickly
In my heart, there is concern
My mind is slow to grasp it
There is an urgency to learn.

Help me understand Your Word
But most of all let me be true
Thankful for this life I live
For it is always about You.

Time is passing so quickly
Looking back can bring sorrow
Oh, don't let me go there Lord
Maybe I'll be here tomorrow.

And if tomorrow comes again
I pray to the Lord to see
Open my heart to serve You
Before You come for me.

Time is passing so quickly
And I hope to use it well
Another day, a gift from You
Only time will tell.

Day 43 – by Stephanie M. White

Ruth 2:11 NIV
Boaz replied, "I've been told all about what you have done for your mother-in-law since the death of your husband..."

Ruth was an example of being rebuilt. Ruth suffered the loss of her husband, but that did not keep Ruth from being a blessing to others.

As we think about Ruth, we can be sure that she grieved. We can imagine the pain she went through and the hard times she encountered. Ruth may have gone through a period of doubt and anxiety. God's Word does not fill us in on the details of her grieving; however, we do see the end result.

Ruth did not let the death of her husband keep her down. I am not saying that this woman suffered loss and got up the very next day and began doing for others; God does not tell us how long she grieved. What we can learn from her is that we can begin to look beyond our pain and embrace life again.

There are times when we may feel guilty for even thinking about moving on and being rebuilt; you may feel guilty right now! I remember going on a work-related vacation without my son; I was guilt-ridden. I did not want to leave him at home and go have fun! Then one day I spoke with him and he was so excited to hear about what I was doing. He was so happy that I was having fun. If our loved ones could speak to us now they would tell us how much joy it would bring them if we would enjoy life again. Again, this does not happen overnight. It is a process, but we must *begin* the process if we are ever going to see this come to pass.

God has great plans for your life! God wants to bless you so that you can be a blessing to others. As you endure this painful time bear in mind that God has a plan to build your life back up! He has an everlasting love for you and He has so many good things in store for you. As you heal, you can begin to be a blessing to others. You can share the comfort you have received from God with others.

Day 44 – by Kathleen Higham
Pray Now

In the moment of rage, I prayed
God helped me through somehow
For He has never failed me yet
Draws me near when my knees bow.

Pray now through the unthinkable
Knowing His Grace is sufficient
God understands our unbelief
We were born to be deficient.

Fearful, naked and screaming, but
Unto life more precious than gold
The Father God prepared the way
For a heart He longs to mold.

Pray now through the unthinkable
Do not meander until tomorrow
Or embrace this chaotic diversion
Then bend to a weighty sorrow.

Pour yourself out and surrender
In humility you feel His Grace
Not to do great things, no
But to stand in a Holy place.

Where He will give you strength
To overcome not questioning how
Fall down be filled with His Glory
Then pray, pray, pray, pray now...

Psalm 73:26
"My flesh and my heart may fail,
But God is the strength of my heart
And my portion forever."

Day 45 – by Stephanie M. White

Isaiah 57:2 KJV
He shall enter into peace: they shall rest in their beds, [each one] walking [in] his uprightness.

As we grieve the loss of our loved ones in this life, we can be encouraged by the rest our loved ones are now enjoying.

God's Word tells us that rest is found in death. The Hebrew word "nuach" was translated as rest. This word has several meanings. One meaning for this word is to settle down. Death takes us to our eternal dwelling place; we settle – we become a resident of heaven if we have received Christ (He is our righteousness – 1 Corinthians 1:30). This word also means to dwell, stay, and remain; heaven is the eternal home of those who have died in Christ. As our loved ones pass from this world, they enter their eternal resting place – their eternal home in heaven!

The Hebrew word "nuach" also means to give comfort. Heaven is a place of eternal relief, ease, and security. Those who pass on enter into peace. They are no longer stressed and anxious; they are tranquil and calm.

Heaven is a place of rest and peace because our dwelling is with God.

> Revelation 21:3 NIV And I heard a loud voice from the throne saying, "Now the dwelling of God is with men, and He will live with them. They will be His people, and God Himself will be with them and be their God."

Heaven is a place of fellowshipping with God. It is a place of peace and rest.

What joy our loved ones are experiencing as they abide in the presence of God! The sorrow that we feel here cannot compare to the joy that we, too, will one day experience with them in our heavenly home.

When times of sadness seem to overtake you, remind yourself of what your loved one is experiencing with God and remind yourself that you will be with them one day soon!

Day 46 – by Kathleen Higham
Shattered

There are times when pain will come
Your heart is completely shattered
You are reaching out to emptiness
Praying, asking God if you ever mattered.

And when these trials overwhelm us
Tears fall down in a flooding rain
It's hard to remember our Jesus
When His body was racked with pain.

But if only you would surrender
Cry out for His mercy, His Word
Close your eyes and open your heart
With compassion His voice will be heard.

For He has given many promises
Knowing how our hearts would grieve
He waits and weeps for our sorrow
Beckoning come to Me and cleave.

This world is filled with the shattered
But as Christians we must believe
The peace and glory of Jesus Christ
Is waiting on the day that we leave.

Oh! I am waiting in joyful hope
For the day when my Lord comes for me
No longer brokenhearted nor shattered
In His arms I will finally be free.

Psalm 147:3

Day 47 – by Stephanie M. White

Ecclesiastes 7:1-2 AMP
A good name is better than precious perfume, and the day of death better than the day of one's birth. It is better to go to the house of mourning than to go to the house of feasting, for that is the end of all men; and the living will lay it to heart.

Solomon describes the day of death as better; it is superior to the day of birth. Death surpasses life; it is to be preferred. This does not mean that we are to hate life here on earth – it means that we are supposed to keep this life in perspective.

This life is temporary and this life comes with its share of problems. In this life, we maintain our sinful nature (flesh); and as a result, we struggle. Our flesh hates the things of the Spirit; it is contrary to the Word of God. Our flesh tries to dominate our mind, our will, our emotions, our actions, and so on, and we have to fight the flesh with the Word of God. This fight becomes monotonous and frustrating at times; albeit, it is well worth it. In heaven, we will no longer experience this struggle. Freedom from our flesh is promised in our eternal dwelling place. Heaven is better!

In heaven, we will no longer be subjected to the concerns of this life. This life, and the trials it brings with it, can be overwhelming at best some days. In heaven, we will be free from the cares of this world – no wonder Solomon describes death as "better!"

Do not forget to remind yourself of all that your loved ones are experiencing in their heavenly home. These thoughts of freedom, peace, security, well-being, joy, and so on, will lighten the load of grief. Our loved ones are in such an amazing place – a place that cannot even be described completely with words.

As those who remain and are awaiting our arrival in our eternal home, we are to lay these thoughts of heaven to heart. Be reminded of the unlimited wonders of your heavenly home. Enjoy thinking of your loved ones in this place of awe!

Day 48 – by Kathleen Higham
Just Say Hello

As Christians we might falter
But one thing we all know
This world is only temporary
A time is coming when we'll go.

A Mansion waits in Heaven
Where every Christian will meet
Flesh fades and spirit lives
Our souls at last complete.

Yet we sometimes fear the future
Not wanting to say good-bye
Suffering will surely grieve us
Saddened eyes release a sigh.

The promise of life everlasting
Oh it seems like a fairy tale
As tired hearts beat heavily
And bodies begin to fail.

No one shall escape this
Hearts cry out, lay bare
Time steals the youth of today
Still we offer God our prayer.

Do not speak of good-bye
For the Lord loves us so
When we finally see Him
He says, "Just Say Hello."

Waiting on the high hills
Just say hello to your friend
Eternal life means no farewells
It is Life, Life without end.

Day 49 – by Stephanie M. White

Genesis 50:1, 3, 7, 10
Joseph threw himself upon his father and wept
over him and kissed him...and the Egyptians
mourned for him seventy days.
So Joseph went up to bury his father...When they
reached the threshing floor of Atad, near the Jordan,
they lamented loudly and bitterly; and there Joseph
observed a seven-day period of mourning for his father.

Joseph's time of mourning was seventy days at first; he also had another time of mourning later on. A season of grief may not be singular; we may experience more than one season of grief. This does not mean we are weak, faithless, or the like. It simply means that we are human.

There will be times in your life that bring back intense memories. Christmas, birthdays, other holidays, and so on, can be just such times. You may have been being rebuilt after a season of grief only to find yourself right back in the throes of mourning. Losing a loved one is a powerfully deep event in your life. One season of grief may not suffice.

If you are experiencing another season of grief do not be hard on yourself. Remember the Word of God; remember God's love. Hold on to what you have learned in the Word of God and focus on God's promises. Bereavement can come in stages. You will never "get over" the person you have lost in this life, but you can learn to move on and look forward to being reunited with them.

Christmas time is a difficult time for my family. My grandma and my uncle passed away and they were such a big part of our Christmas celebration. We miss having them with us, but we do talk and laugh about the times we have had with them. There will be certain times that are harder than others. There will be places and things that intensify your feeling of grief. If you encounter another season of grief, keep your focus on the Word of God! He will take you through as many times as you need Him to!

Day 50 – by Kathleen Higham
Even After the Sun Has Set

---Relay for Life 2012---

Written for those who are still in the race and remembering those who have now seen His face...

It is a cold, dark and rainy morning. Yesterday was a beautiful, warm and sunny day as we walked in Mill Creek Park. My thoughts raced inside my mind and time was running through me at a maddening pace. For just a few days ago a sweet friend had lost the race. She was only fifty-five years old. I can't help but wonder why such a lovely person would die so suddenly leaving behind two teenagers who needed her. She battled breast cancer and bone cancer for over four years. Then, without warning, she was struck down by a heart attack at her place of work. Unknowing, I went to see her. Her personal belongings sat on her desk. Her pillow still rested against her chair, but my friend was no longer there. There have been many tragic events this year, but this was the most sobering moment of disbelief; grief would come later, along with the realization of the fragile state of one's immortality. Now the profound disappointment comes not because my life is near completion, but for the devastated faces of those loved ones. I felt disappointment for the total ignorance of some who are so blessed by God; yet, they take this life for granted believing tomorrow actually exists. And even more shocking, they believe they have earned the right to another day. When one grows older the gift comes in acknowledging, "the gift..." We have not earned one thing, nor are we promised the elusive tomorrow. If we wake up, so be it. He saw it fit. This morning I reach for my notebook and my pencil in thankfulness. Should God allow me to finish this piece, or shall my pencil fall silently to the floor, to write no more. It is certainly a possibility and brings a very important revelation as one ages. We have no tomorrow; we have only this moment. If you stand before the sunset for another night, you must praise God for the blessed sight. But most of all, give to Him your heart and soul in the last hour before the night. If you have loved God with all your might, then give to Him the one hour before the inky black sky closes over you. This could be the very last sunset you shall ever see. Give thanks for your life before unbeknownst, it should flee. Dear ones, there is time if you would recognize what God will do. For your loved ones, He glorified your name and left behind the sweetest memories of you. He is thoughtfully kind to leave behind---Surely not a world of promises to come day after day---No! This life shall end and in the final hour the earthly light shall fade away. What will you say? "Remember me." Oh precious one, remember Him, and what He lovingly designed. This is what our Lord would do. Even after the sun has set---Your loved ones will remember you...

Even after the sun has set
Darkness does not claim the sky
It waits and hovers in wonder
For God to close its eye.

There is much to do dear ones
And there is even more to find
To Him, give your heart and soul
Then who you are will be defined.

Now the hour of this beautiful day
For many will have just begun
But oh so quickly it is gone
When to the West, sets the sun.

Thousands gone down in silence
On a dark haired child of yesterday
From a babe in a mother's arms
To the one growing old and grey.

Yet there is time between the sunset
I believe, an hour, they say
Don't waste one precious moment
Fall to your knees and pray.

And if into an inky black sky
Your prayers seem to slip away
Do not worry for God holds them
As He waits for the glorious day.

When the final sunset drifts slowly down
God remembers the hour of your birth
And from the darkness to the light
He will sweep you from this earth.

Oh glory comes from the Father
Unimaginable what He has designed
Because you gave your heart and soul
Sweet memories of you were left behind.

Even after the sun has set
There is nothing our Lord won't do
Even after the sun has set
Your loved ones will remember you...

More devotionals by Stephanie and Kathleen:

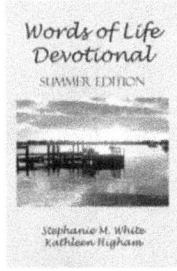

**Words of Life Devotional
Summer Edition**

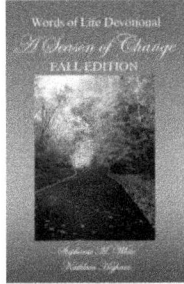

**Words of Life Devotional
Fall Edition**

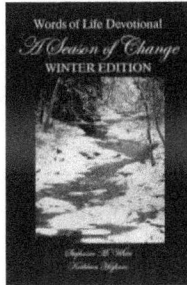

**Words of Life Devotional
Winter Edition**

www.heavenonearthforme.com

A NEW BEGINNING

This devotional is for those who are new to the Word and their walk with God.

www.heavenonearthforme.com

For more information on poetry by Kathleen Higham, please contact her at:

kathleenhigham@yahoo.com

More books by Stephanie White:

HEAVEN ON EARTH: it is a life most people believe is not possible to achieve, but according to God's Word that is exactly what we can have! Heaven on Earth takes you on a journey through the Word of God so that you can find out what is available to you as God's child and you will also discover how to enjoy this life to the fullest.

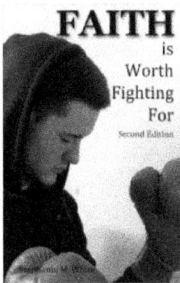

FAITH IS WORTH FIGHTING FOR: In God's Word we discover that we are to live by faith, but we also see that faith is a fight. As a Christian, faith is essential. Eternal value is assigned to our faith. This book is an in-depth study of faith - what faith is, how we obtain it, how it works, what classifies it as genuine, what its benefits are, and more.

www.heavenonearthforme.com

More books by Stephanie White:

THE TWO OF ME: As Christians, we must understand that we have two natures - our Spiritual nature and our flesh. Each nature wants to dominate, but only one can. This book will take you through a thorough study of your two natures and it will help you understand each one. It will also show you how to rule over your flesh and defeat its power in your life.

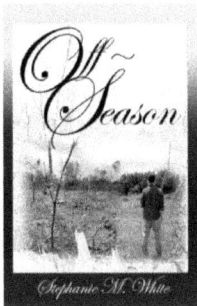

OFF-SEASON Everyone experiences an off-season in life - sometimes more than one. An off-season is a dry time; it is a time of lack and a time of trials. These times can feel daunting and painful; therefore, we must understand the purpose of these times and we must be sure that God has a plan for our good and His glory

www.heavenonearthforme.com

www.ingramcontent.com/pod-product-compliance
Lightning Source LLC
Chambersburg PA
CBHW051045030426

42339CB00006B/208